Ducks

Ducks

Mary Ann McDonald

THE CHILD'S WORLD, INC.

Library of Congress Cataloging-in-Publication Data
McDonald, Mary Ann.
Ducks/written by Mary Ann McDonald.
p.   cm.
Includes index.
Summary: Introduces the physical characteristics, behavior, and life cycle of ducks.
ISBN 1-56766-376-1 (alk. paper)
1. Ducks—Juvenile literature. [1. Ducks.] I. Title.
QL696.A52M385   1997
598.4'1—dc21   96-46138
CIP
AC

Photo Credits

Art Wolfe/Tony Stone Images:10
COMSTOCK/Art Gingert: 2. 29
COMSTOCK/COMSTOCK, Inc: 6, 9
COMSTOCK/Denver Bryan: 16
COMSTOCK/Dr. Rose K. Gantner: 20
COMSTOCK.Gary Benson: 23
COMSTOCK/R. Michael Stuckey: cover
COMSTOCK/Russ Kinne: 26
COMSTOCK/S. Chester: 19
COMSTOCK/Townshend P. Dickinson: 24
Gary Meszaros/DEMBINSKY PHOTO ASSOC: 15
Joe McDonald: 30
Leonard Lee Rue III/Tony Stone Images: 13

On the cover...

Front cover: This *ringed teal duck* is standing by a pond.
Page 2: *Mandarin ducks* like this one are brightly colored.

Table of Contents

Chapter	Page

Imagine that you are sitting by a pond on a sunny spring day. You see lots of creatures eating and playing around the pond. Near the shore, turtles sit on a brown log. Frogs croak on green lily pads. But soon you notice an animal farther out in the water. It seems very happy swimming around in the pond. After taking a closer look, you see that the animal is a bird. What could it be? It's a duck!

Mallard ducks like this one like to swim in ponds.

Ducks are **waterfowl**, or birds that live around water. Swans and geese are also waterfowl. Waterfowl fly just like other birds, but they can also swim and float. Like most waterfowl, ducks are found in the wild. But sometimes ducks are raised by people.

These *spectacled eider ducks* are very colorful.

A male duck is called a **drake**. Drakes are usually very colorful. Some drakes have bright green heads and curly tails. Others have colorful stripes on their wings.

A female duck is called a **hen**. Hens aren't as bright and colorful as drakes. Most of them are a plain, dark color such as brown. This coloring helps the hens hide from enemies while they are nesting.

This mallard drake and hen are standing by a river.

Ducks have two feet that are perfect for swimming. Between a duck's toes there are flaps of skin called **webs**. The webs turn the duck's feet into flippers. These flippers push the duck quickly through the water. With the help of their webbed feet, some ducks even dive underwater to look for food.

The webs of this *black-bellied whistling in tree duck* are pink.

Do All Ducks Look the Same?

There are many different kinds of ducks. *Pintails* are medium-sized ducks with long, pointed tails. *Wood ducks* have bright green feathers that stick up on their heads. *Ring-billed ducks* have white stripes on their beaks. And one kind of farmyard duck, called a *Pekin duck*, has bright orange feet!

Many people think *wood ducks* like this one are very beautiful.

Where Do Ducks Build Their Nests?

Like other birds, ducks sit on their eggs. And just like songbirds, ducks like to be far away from people and other animals when they nest. Most ducks make their nests on the ground. But some ducks find other places to nest. Duck nests have been found under bushes, in hollow trees, and even inside doghouses!

These duck eggs are safely hidden in the weeds.

What Are Baby Ducks Like?

Once a hen has found a safe, quiet spot to build her nest, she starts laying eggs. She lays one egg a day for most of the spring and summer. Some ducks lay as many as 200 eggs in one year! When a baby duck hatches, it is called a **duckling**. Most ducklings are brown, just like the ground and grass they live in. This coloring helps them hide from enemies. After several months, the ducklings grow their adult feathers, or **plumage**.

Most ducklings have dark colors like this one.

Ducks eat many different things. Some eat small fish, baby frogs, and insects. Others like corn or bread as a treat. Most ducks eat grasses and tiny plants that live in water. But how do the ducks eat these plants?

This *Mandarin duck* is eating water plants.

All ducks have a special beak called a **bill**. A duck's bill is much rounder and flatter than a songbird's beak. The duck uses its bill to scoop up mouthfuls of water. The water drains out the sides of the bill, leaving the tiny plants behind. Now the duck can eat the plants without having to drink all of the water too!

Pekin ducks like this one have bright orange bills.

Ducks can't chew their food, because they don't have any teeth. Instead, they swallow sand or small stones they find on the ground. These little stones are called **grit**. The grit sits in a special stomach called a **gizzard**. When the duck eats, the food goes to the gizzard first. The grit in the gizzard grinds the food into tiny pieces. Then the food is ready to travel on to the main stomach.

These mallards are searching for grit in the mud.

Ducks have a special oil on their outer feathers. This oil keeps them dry and helps them float on water. The oil comes from a spot near the base of the duck's tail. The duck spreads the oil when it cleans, or **preens** its feathers. A duck preens almost every time it comes out of the water.

This mallard's wing is shiny and clean after preening.

Ducks also have a special layer of feathers right next to their skin. These feathers, called **down**, keep the ducks warm in cold weather. Down is very soft and fluffy. Many people use down in pillows and jackets because it is so soft and warm.

This female wood duck has used her own down to make her nest soft and warm.

So the next time you are on a farm or at a local park, look for ducks. Can you tell if they are mallards or pintails? Take along some cracked corn to feed them. You'll soon be surrounded by some very friendly ducks!

This male Mandarin duck is watching over his pond.

Glossary

bill (BILL)
The beak of a duck is called a bill. A duck's bill is flat with a rounded end.

down (DOWN)
Down is a layer of soft, fluffy feathers found next to a duck's skin. These feathers keep the duck warm.

drake (DRAKE)
A male duck is a drake. Many drakes are colorful.

ducklings (DUK-lings)
Ducklings are baby ducks. Ducklings are soft and fluffy.

gizzard (GIH-zerd)
A gizzard is a special stomach. The gizzard holds small stones that grind up food.

grit (GRIT)
Grit is sand or small stones that a duck swallows. The grit grinds up food in the duck's gizzard.

hen (HEN)
A female duck is a hen. Most hens have plain coloring that helps them hide from enemies.

plumage (PLOO-mij)
An adult bird's feathers are called its plumage. Many ducks have colorful plumage.

preen (PREEN)
When a duck preens, it cleans and oils its feathers. The oil keeps the feathers waterproof.

waterfowl (WA-tur-FOWL)
Waterfowl are birds that live around the water. Ducks, geese, and swans are all waterfowl.

webs (WEBZ)
The flaps of skin between a duck's toes are called webs. The webs help the duck swim quickly through the water.

Index